Unit 1 Tell me about it

Listening comprehension

1 You will hear three people calling a housing agent about three different houses. Listen to their conversations and complete the information in the table by placing a tick ☑, a cross ☒ or a number, in each column.

	Number of bedrooms	Living-room: large	Living-room: small	Dining-room	Garage	Garden: large	Garden: small	Rent
1								
2								
3								

2 You will hear someone talking to a landlord about two different apartments. Listen to their conversations and mark on the list ☑ the contents of each apartment.

	14 Sutton Place	75 Glenwood Drive
Sofa	....	....
Dining-table	....	....
Bookshelves	....	....
TV	....	....
Carpets	....	....
Curtains	....	....
Beds	....	....
Mattresses	....	....
Refrigerator	....	....
Air-conditioners	....	....

Conversation exercises

1 Choose the most suitable answer and write it out.

1 **A** Are there any curtains in the house?

   B ....

   No, it hasn't.
   No, there are.
   No, there aren't.

2 **A** How big is the apartment?

   B ....

   Oh, quite small.
   Yes, very big.
   No, quite small.

3 **A** What sort of house is it?

   B ....

   An apartment block.
   A terraced house.
   Near a park.

4 **A** What are the grounds like?

   B ....

   No, there isn't.
   It's very small.
   They're quite large.

5 **A** What's the neighbourhood like?

   B ....

   It's near by.
   It's very friendly.
   They are nice.

2 Write true answers to these questions about your residence.

1 **A** What sort of house or apartment do you live in?

   B I live ....

2 **A** How many rooms are there in it altogether? (name them)

   B .... , altogether: ....

   ....

3 **A** Is there a garden around your house/apartment?

   B ....

4 **A** How close do you live to a bus route?

   B ....

5 **A** Are there any shops near by? How far away are they and what sort of shops are they?

   B ....

   ....

6 **A** What do you like most about your neighbourhood?

   B ....

   ....

Grammar review

1 Use the words given to write answers to these questions. Use either *Yes, there is one in...* or *Yes, there are some in....*

1 Are there any knives and forks? (the kitchen cupboard)

   ....

2 Is there a telephone? (the bedroom)

   ....

3 Are there any bookshelves? (the dining-room)

   ....

4 Is there a television? (the living-room)

   ....

5 Is there a writing desk? (the bedroom)

   ....

6 Are there any carpets? (the bedrooms)

   ....

2 Provide the questions to these answers.

1 ....?

   It's got six rooms altogether.

2 ....?

   No, it's got a combined living and dining-room.

3 ....?

   Yes, it's got quite a big garden.

4 ....?

   It's only half an hour away from the centre of town.

5 ....?

   Yes, there are some good shops just down the street.

6 ....?

   Yes, it's a very pleasant neighbourhood to live in.

7 ....?

   Yes, there's an excellent bus system to the centre of town.

Writing

Read this advertisement from the newspaper.

> 45 Ford Drive. 3 bedroom family home, double garage. New condition. Large garden. Short walk to city centre and schools. $74,000.

Now read this paragraph, which is based on the advertisement.

> There is a 3 bedroom family home for sale at 45 Ford Drive. It has a double garage and the house is in new condition. It is a short walk from the house to the city centre and the schools. The price is $74,000.

Write paragraphs like this based on the advertisements below.

1. 56 Grace St. Modern 2 storey 6 bedroom home, large living-room, separate dining-room, 3 bathrooms, basement, garage. Beautiful garden and swimming-pool. Excellent condition. $150,000.

2. Lindon St. Attractive 3 bedroom family home; dining-room, living-room, 2 bathrooms. Opposite bus-stop, 5 mnts from twn. Brick construction. Small garden, 2 car garage. $80,000.

3. Crowley St. New 1 bedroom apt. 10th floor. Furnished. Good view. Refrigerator, new stove, air-con. Close to shops. $25,000.

Unit 2 What's the difference?

Listening comprehension

1 You will hear a customer talking to a salesperson about three watches. Listen to their conversation and complete the information in the table below.

	Smallest	Biggest	Cheapest	Heaviest
Seiko				
Citizen				
Pulsar				

2 You will hear a customer talking to a salesperson about some typewriters. Listen to their conversation and complete the information in the table below.

	Price	Country of manufacture	Period of guarantee	The best made machine
Brother				
Adler				
Corona				
IBM				

3 You will hear two people talking to Patrick about his brothers and sisters. Listen to their conversation and write down the age of each person.

Name	Age
Pat	....
Terry	....
Dick	....
Anne	....
Jane	....
Sue	....

Grammar review

1 Write comments to these statements using this model.

1 This coat is too small.
   I'll bring you a bigger one.

2 This ring is too expensive.
   ....

3 This bag is too heavy.
   ....

4 This jacket is not big enough.
   ....

5 This watch is too light.
   ....

6 This skirt is too wide.
   ....

7 This belt is too thick.
   ....

2 Write answers to these questions. The first one is done for you.

1 What's the largest city in Japan?
   Tokyo is the largest.

2 What's the tallest mountain in the world?
   ....

3 What's the best hotel in your city?
   ....

4 What's the warmest month in your country?
   ....

5 Who's the most famous pop singer in your country?
   ....

6 Who's the most popular actor?
   ....

7 What's the best tourist resort in your country?
   ....

3 Write answers to these questions using this model.

1 Which is more expensive: a Rolex or a Citizen?
   A Rolex is more expensive .

2 Which month is cooler in your country: June or December?

3 Which is more economical: a large car or a small one?

4 Which do you think is tastier: Western food or Asian food?

5 Which is more expensive: a Cadillac or a Toyota?

6 Which is easier to drive: an automatic car or a manual one?

7 Which is lighter: a leather coat or a woollen one?

8 Which is more comfortable: a bus ride or a train ride?

4 Write answers to these questions using this model.

1 Do you like Western food?
   No, I like Asian food better.

2 Do you like classical music?

3 Do you like war films?

4 Do you like playing chess?

5 Do you like studying English?

6 Do you like Italian food?

7 Do you like reading magazines?

Writing

Read this paragraph about the Smith family.

The Smiths

The Smiths have a very large family. There are seven in the family altogether, two boys and three girls. Harry is the oldest child. He is eighteen. The next oldest is Paul. He is fifteen. After that comes Anne. She is twelve. Then there is Suzanne. She is nine. Sally is the youngest in the family. She is five.

Write paragraphs like this about these families. Use *quite a large family..., quite a small....*

The Robinsons

1 ....
....
....
....

The Grants

2 ....
....
....
....

Unit 3 What does it look like?

Listening comprehension

1 You will hear descriptions of three different watches. Listen to each description and write the correct number below the picture.

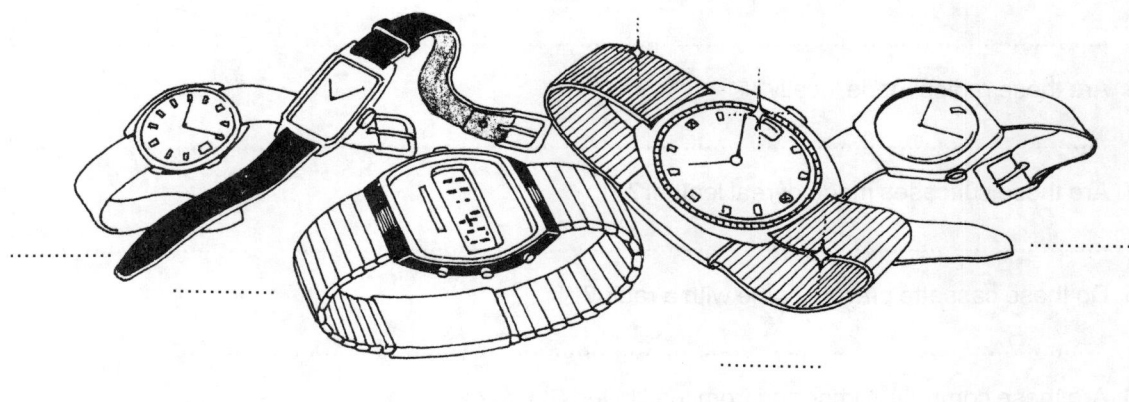

2 You will hear people calling to enquire about the items in the table which have been advertised for sale in the newspaper. Listen to their conversations and complete the information in the table.

		Age in years	Condition	Size	Price
1	Refrigerator				
2	Television				
3	Wall unit				
4	Desk				

3 You will hear Mrs Lodge talking to her friend about her children, Anne and Peter. Listen to their conversation, then complete the table below by placing a tick ☑ or a cross ☒ in each column.

	Anne	Peter
Study at university		
Live at home		
Graduate this year		
Like sport		
Drive their own car		

Grammar review

1 Write positive or negative replies to these questions using *Yes, all of them are/do* or *No, none of them are/do*. Use the cues given for a positive ⊞ or negative ⊠ reply.

1 Are these pens made of stainless steel? ⊞

....

2 Do these television sets come with a guarantee? ⊞

....

3 Are these radios made locally? ⊠

....

4 Are these suitcases made of real leather? ⊠

....

5 Do these cassette players come with a radio? ⊠

....

6 Are these computers imported from the United States? ⊠

....

2 This time reply to these questions with *Yes, both of them are/do* or *No, neither of them are/do*. Use the cues given for a positive ⊞ or negative ⊠ reply.

1 Are these watches made in Japan? ⊞

....

2 Do these pens come with a guarantee? ⊞

....

3 Are these television sets colour? ⊠

....

4 Do these TV sets cost over $500? ⊠

....

5 Are these suitcases made of real leather? ⊞

....

6 Do these bags have a combination lock? ⊠

....

7 Are these record-players made in Hong Kong? ⊞

....

3 Look at this table.

	Bob	John	Pam	Jane
Goes to university	✓		✓	
Speaks a foreign language	✓		✓	✓
Plays tennis well		✓		✓
Likes swimming	✓			
Has a driving-licence		✓	✓	
Owns a car		✓		
Knows how to type				✓
Likes cooking	✓		✓	

Write answers to these questions about Bob, John, Pam and Jane using *All of them...*, *None of them...*, *Bob and Pam...*, *Jane...*, etc., adding a suitable verb (*do, does, is, are*).

1 Which of them go to university?

....

2 Do any of them speak a foreign language?

....

3 Are any of them good at tennis?

....

4 Do they all like swimming?

....

5 Do any of them have a driving-licence?

....

6 Are any of them owners of a car?

....

4 Now compare John and Jane only. Answer these questions.

1 Do either of them speak a foreign language?

....

2 Which of them knows how to type?

....

3 Are either of them good at tennis?

....

4 Are they good at cooking?

....

Writing

Read this description of a watch which someone wants to sell.

> For sale. A ladies Citizen watch. This is a nearly new automatic watch in very good condition, with a gold metal strap.

Write 'For Sale' descriptions like this of the things below, using the information given.

1. Writing desk, 4' by 3', metal, two drawers; 4 years old; good condition (slight scratch on one leg).

   ....
   ....
   ....

2. Typewriter (portable, electric), Japanese; 3 years old, with case. Also, small typing desk—wooden; good condition, but needs minor repairs.

   ....
   ....
   ....

3. Camera (Nikon 35mm) with 3 rolls film, two extra lenses; 6 months old.

   ....
   ....
   ....

4. Wall unit; 6' × 6', wood, contains bookshelves, drawers, stereo and radio compartments; 3 years old (but looks new); cheap price.

   ....
   ....
   ....

5. Set of dining-room furniture; sofa (new covering—light green), four chairs (wooden), small round table (glass); sofa nearly new; chairs 3 years old; all excellent condition.

   ....
   ....
   ....

Unit 4 What are you going to do?

Listening comprehension

1 You will hear someone talking to Mr Roberts about his children Frank, Herbert and Elizabeth. Listen to their conversation and mark whether the statements below are TRUE ☑ or FALSE ☒.

1 Frank is a college student. TRUE ☐ FALSE ☐
2 Frank wants to be a lawyer. TRUE ☐ FALSE ☐
3 He had an interview with a law firm last week. TRUE ☐ FALSE ☐
4 Frank is travelling to Westview shortly. TRUE ☐ FALSE ☐
5 Herbert is going to graduate from high school very shortly. TRUE ☐ FALSE ☐
6 Herbert isn't going to go to university. TRUE ☐ FALSE ☐
7 Herbert is going to get a job as a salesman. TRUE ☐ FALSE ☐
8 Elizabeth just got married. TRUE ☐ FALSE ☐
9 She and her husband are going to go away shortly. TRUE ☐ FALSE ☐

2 Jenny is going on a vacation shortly. A friend is talking to her about her holiday plans. Listen to their conversation and complete the information below.

1 The country Jenny is going to: ....
2 The day she is leaving: ....
3 The number of days she will be there: ....
4 Where she is going to stay: ....
5 What she will do there: ....
6 The season there at this time of year: ....
7 The airline she is travelling on: ....
8 The time of her departure: ....

3 You will hear two friends talking about their weekend plans. Listen to their conversation and complete the table below with brief notes about what they are going to do, (e.g. going shopping, watching TV).

	Friday night	Saturday	Sunday
Jim			
Gillian			

Conversation exercises

Choose the most suitable answer and write it out.

1 **A** How have you been? | Oh, not much.
   B .... | How are you?
   | Fine, thanks.

2 **A** Are you doing anything tonight? | I haven't got anything
   B .... | planned.
   | No, thanks.
   | Not at all.

3 **A** How about coming to a movie? | Fine, thanks.
   B .... | Sorry, I'm not free.
   | Yes, I will.

4 **A** How long are you going to be away? | On Monday.
   B .... | Since Thursday.
   | Not for long.

5 **A** What about going out for dinner? | That sounds fun.
   B .... | Yes, I will.
   | Not much.

Grammar review

1 Find another way of expressing each question or statement. The first one is done for you.

   1 What are you doing on Saturday night?
   Are you doing anything on Saturday night?

   OR
   What are you going to do on Saturday night?

   2 When are you leaving for your vacation?
   ....

   3 I'm leaving on Thursday.
   ....

   4 How have you been lately?
   ....

   5 How about coming to a movie with us?
   ....

   6 Oh, that would be great, but I'm not free on Sunday.
   ....

2 Write negative responses to these questions adding suitable information. The first one is done for you.

1 Are you going to be home on Saturday afternoon? *No, I'm not going to be home.*
I'm going to play tennis.

2 Are you going to be home tomorrow night? ....

3 Are you going to be home on Sunday? ....

4 Are you going to be home tonight? ....

5 Are you going to be home on Saturday morning? ....

6 Are you going to be home on Wednesday night? ....

7 Are you going to be home in the weekend? ....

3 Write suitable answers to these questions.

1 Where are you studying at the moment?
I'm studying at Freyberg High School.

2 What English course are you taking?
....

3 What English book are you studying from?
....

4 Where are you living at the moment?
....

5 What company are you working for?
....

6 What section are you working in?
....

7 What courses are you taking this year?
....

Writing

Read this itinerary for Miss Judy Lucas's visit to the United States.

Miss J. Lucas US ITINERARY

July 4   Arrive Los Angeles
         Visit Disneyland, MGM Film Studio
         Stay Hilton Hotel
July 7   Los Angeles—San Francisco
         Visit Golden Gate Bridge, Japanese Garden, Fisherman's Wharf
         Stay Tremont Hotel
July 9   San Francisco—Chicago
         City tour, night-club tour, museum tour
         Stay Foster Hotel
July 11 Chicago—New York
         Manhattan tour, boat trip around Long Island, see UN Building,
         Empire State Building, Metropolitan Opera
         Stay Redford Hotel

Write a description of Miss Lucas's visit, based on the information above.

Miss Judy Lucas is arriving in Los Angeles on July the 4th.
In Los Angeles, she's going to

Unit 5   This is what I want you to do

Listening comprehension

1. Listen to the conversation between Mrs Green and Henry and put a tick ☑ beside the things that Henry has to do.
   - ☐ Buy some eggs
   - ☐ Get some milk
   - ☐ Buy some fruit
   - ☐ Get some white bread
   - ☐ Get some brown bread
   - ☐ Collect the dry-cleaning
   - ☐ Take the clothes to the dry-cleaners
   - ☐ Buy some airmail envelopes
   - ☐ Buy some white envelopes

2. Jane is helping her friend Anne tidy the house. Listen to their conversation and put a tick ☑ to show in which room each item belongs.

	Kitchen	Living-room	Bedroom 1	Bedroom 2	Bedroom 3
magazines					
glasses					
red slippers					
dictionary					
shirts					
vase					
wastepaper-basket					
cushions					

3. You will be told how to draw shapes in the two squares. Listen and follow the instructions you hear.

   1.

   2.

Grammar review

1 Rewrite these questions more politely using *Would you...*, *Could you...*, or *Will you...please....*

1 Put away the books and magazines.
   ....

2 Type this letter for me.
   ....

3 Take these letters to the post office.
   ....

4 Gift wrap that for me.
   ....

5 Get me some fruit at the supermarket.
   ....

6 Give me a dozen eggs.
   ....

7 Put these sheets in the washing-machine.
   ....

2 Write replies to these questions using *I'd like you to...* and suggesting suitable places to put each item. The first one is done for you.

1 Where shall I put these glasses?
   I'd like you to put them in the kitchen.

2 Where shall I put these books?
   ....

3 Where shall I put these knives and forks?
   ....

4 Where shall I put the milk?
   ....

5 Where shall I put the waste-paper basket?
   ....

6 Where shall I put these flowers?
   ....

3 Choose one of the alternatives given to answer these questions. The first one is done for you.

1 Do you want me to send these letters airmail or surface mail?
Send them surface mail, please.

2 Do you want me to get airmail envelopes or plain ones?
....

3 Do you want me to get beef or chicken at the supermarket?
....

4 Do you want me to wash the dishes or vacuum the carpet?
....

5 Do you want me to wash this shirt in hot or in warm water?
....

6 Do you want me to trim your hair or to cut it short?
....

7 Do you want me to get fruit juice or soft drink?
....

4 Choose *It goes...* or *They go...* and suggest a place in the kitchen where each thing might go (e.g. in the cupboard next to the shelf; in the drawer near the sink; on the top shelf; in the refrigerator; in the middle drawer; in the cupboard, etc.).

1 Where does the sugar go? ....
....

2 Where do the eggs go? ....
....

3 Where do these napkins go? ....
....

4 Where does the salt go? ....
....

5 Where do the vegetables go? ....
....

6 Where do these plates go? ....
....

7 Where does the fruit go? ....
....

Writing

Mr Harris's gardener is coming to do some work in Mr Harris's garden. Read this note to the gardener.

> Pedro,
> Here's what I'd like you to do today. First, pick up the leaves and mow the lawn. Then cut the hedge at the front of the house. After that (if you have time), please tidy the flower garden at the back of the house.

Write notes like this using the information below.

1. Mrs Grant wants her cleaning lady (Mrs Santos) to take all the sheets off the beds and wash them; to vacuum the carpets and to clean the kitchen and the bathroom.

   ....
   ....
   ....
   ....

2. Mrs Jamison wants her secretary (Jane) to prepare the pay envelopes for the staff; to make three copies of the annual report; to type the letters in the out-tray and to finish filing the sales reports.

   ....
   ....
   ....
   ....

3. Mr Dakin wants his assistant (John) to take the company car in for servicing; to collect the Glaxo contract from the lawyers; to make the reservations for Mr Dakin's trip to Europe and to try to arrange an appointment with Mr Dakin's doctor.

   ....
   ....
   ....
   ....

4. Mrs Rogerson wants her sons to water the plants when they come home from school; to feed the cats; to tidy their room.

   ....
   ....
   ....
   ....

Unit 6 Tell me about yourself

Listening comprehension

1 You will hear Karen being interviewed for a job. Mark on the list below the things that are TRUE (write T) or FALSE (write F).

   1 She majored in business administration. ....
   2 She didn't take any courses in computer science. ....
   3 She didn't take any law courses. ....
   4 She can type well. ....
   5 She speaks French well. ....
   6 She speaks Spanish well. ....
   7 She writes Spanish well. ....
   8 She is interested in business. ....
   9 She has had a lot of practical experience in business. ....

2 You will hear Teresa, Wendy and Michael being interviewed for a job. Each person will be interviewed for one of the positions advertised below. Listen to each interview and then write the person's name beneath the position you think he or she applied for.

Art assistant needed to work in advertising agency. High school diploma and technical drawing skills needed. Tel. 6733.	Salesperson to work in the women's clothing section of a large department store. Good knowledge of English needed. Tel. 52356.
....	....
Vacancy for salesperson in motor company showroom. No previous experience needed, but successful applicant must possess driving-licence. Tel. 2553.	Publishing house seeks a proofreader for educational books. Good command of English essential. No previous experience required. Tel. 553071.
....	....
Immediate vacancy. Clerk to work in office of foreign export company. Knowledge of business procedures essential. Good opportunities for promotion. Tel. 9335.	Insurance company seeks secretary to work in our head office. Previous experience an advantage. Tel. 54890
....	

Conversation exercises

Choose the most suitable answer and write it out.

1 **A** Are you good at languages?　　　　　　　　　　　　　Quite well.
　　　　　　　　　　　　　　　　　　　　　　　　　　　　　　No, not really.
　B ....　　No, I don't.

2 **A** How well do you speak English?　　　　　　　　　　　Too well.
　　　　　　　　　　　　　　　　　　　　　　　　　　　　　　That well.
　B ....　　Reasonably well.

3 **A** How good is your written English?　　　　　　　　　　Quite good.
　　　　　　　　　　　　　　　　　　　　　　　　　　　　　　Very well.
　B ....　　Not at all.

4 **A** Do you know anything about computers?　　　　　　　All right.
　　　　　　　　　　　　　　　　　　　　　　　　　　　　　　Not very well.
　B ....　　Not very much.

5 **A** Do you type very well?　　　　　　　　　　　　　　　Not too badly.
　　　　　　　　　　　　　　　　　　　　　　　　　　　　　　No, I can't.
　B ....　　Not much.

Grammar review

1 Write each question in another way. The first one is done for you.

　1 Do you know a lot about maths?
　　Are you good at maths?
　　..

　2 Do you know much about management?

　　..

　3 How good is your spoken English?

　　..

　4 When can you come for an appointment?

　　..

　5 What's your written English like?

　　..

　6 Can you type well?

　　..

　7 Do you like reading?

　　..

2 Write answers to these questions using the phrases given. The first one is done for you.

1 How well do you speak English? (pretty well)
I speak English pretty well.

2 How well can you type? (quite well)
....

3 How well can you swim? (very well)
....

4 How well do you play tennis? (quite well)
....

3 This time write negative replies.

1 Do you swim well? (very well)
No, I don't swim very well.

2 Can you type well? (at all well)
....

3 How well can you draw? (at all)
....

4 How well can you speak French? (very well)
....

4 Write answers to these questions using the phrases given.

1 Are you good at maths? (quite good)
Yes, I'm quite good at it.

2 What are you like at statistics? (reasonably good)
....

3 What are you like at typing? (OK)
....

4 Are you good at spelling? (pretty good)
....

5 What's your English pronunciation like? (not too bad)
....

6 Are you good at writing essays? (quite good)
....

Writing

Read this advertisement.

> **MORNING POST** 6 JUNE
> **Vacancy**
> We have a vacancy for a salesperson. This is an interesting position for someone with a good knowledge of English and with an interest in meeting people. Write to P.O. Box 35, Brother Typewriters Ltd.

Read Fiona's letter of application for the above position.

> Brother Typewriters Ltd,
> P.O. Box 35
>
> Dear Sirs,
>   I would like to apply for the position of salesperson advertised in the Morning Post on June 6.
>   I am 20 years old. I graduated from Westport High School in March of this year. At school I took English, Maths, Business Studies, Typing and History.
>   I am very interested in sales work and I am sure I would be able to help increase the sales of your company's products.
>   I would be able to start work at the end of the month and I could come for an interview at any time. Thank you for your consideration.
>
> Yours sincerely,
> *Fiona Castle*
> Fiona Castle

Write a letter like this applying for the position above. Put your address and the date at the top of the letter. Give true information about yourself and your educational background. Give additional information about why you think you would be good for the position.

....
....
....
....
....
....
....
....
....
....
....

Unit 7 What were you doing?

Listening comprehension

1 You will hear conversations in which people talk about different incidents. Mark ☑ the correct reason for each incident.
   1 a The dog caused the stain on the carpet. ☐
      b A child spilt something on the carpet last night. ☐
      c It was caused during the children's party. ☐
      d A dinner guest spilt something on the carpet. ☐

   2 a Mr Harris scratched his car going into the parking lot. ☐
      b He scratched the car at his home. ☐
      c Someone scratched the car with a knife. ☐

   3 a The truck was travelling very fast. ☐
      b The rest of the traffic was moving very quickly. ☐
      c The car was coming out of a side street. ☐

2 You will hear a person describe someone they saw commit a robbery. Listen to their description and complete the information in the table below.

   1 The robber's age   ....   7 Colour of shirt   ....
   2 His height   ....   8 Wearing a jacket?   ....
   3 His hair colour   ....   9 Colour of trousers   ....
   4 Length of hair   ....   10 Wearing shoes?   ....
   5 Wearing glasses?   ....   11 Carrying anything?   ....
   6 Wearing a cap?   ....

3 You will hear a description of the people in the picture below. Listen to the description and write the correct number beside each person's picture.
   1 Mr Lewis
   2 Mr King
   3 Mr Young
   4 Mr North
   5 Mr Peters

25

Grammar review

1 Write answers to these questions using the phrases given and this model.

1. What happened to your foot? (twist/playing tennis)
   I twisted it while I was playing tennis.

2. What did you do to your foot? (sprain/playing football)
   ....

3. What did you do to your arm? (burnt/cooking)
   ....

4. How did you hurt your eye? (scratch/swimming)
   ....

5. What happened to your leg? (broke/skiing)
   ....

6. What did you do to your finger? (cut/gardening)
   ....

7. How did you hurt your arm? (sprain/playing basketball)
   ....

2 Join these sentences using this model.

1. Mary was cleaning the vase. She dropped it.
   While Mary was cleaning the vase she dropped it.

2. John was driving home. He had an accident.
   ....

3. Penny was cooking dinner. The guests arrived.
   ....

4. Brian was ironing his shirt. He burnt it.
   ....

5. The children were playing. They broke the window.
   ....

6. Kim was parking the car. She damaged it.
   ....

7. Mrs Scott was cleaning the vase. She broke it.
   ....

Writing

1 Look at the people in the picture and write a sentence about each person. Identify each person by describing what he/she is wearing when the picture was taken, where he/she was sitting, what he/she was doing, etc. The first one is done for you.

1 Miss Martin
2 Mr Fox
3 Miss Leslie
4 Mrs Grant
5 Mrs Leigh
6 Miss Stevens
7 Mr Long
8 Miss Jenkins
9 Mr Harris

1 *The woman who was standing near the window wearing a black dress was Miss Martin.*

2 ....

3 ....

4 ....

5 ....

6 ....

7 ....

8 ....

9 ....

2 You saw these people leaving the scene of a robbery. Write a brief description of each person giving as much information as you can about them. The first one is done for you.

1 *The first man was very young. He was quite tall. He had long hair and he was wearing a scarf. He wasn't wearing glasses. He was wearing a dark sweater and dark trousers. He was wearing sandals. He was carrying a torch.*

2 ....

3 ....

4 ....

5 ....

Unit 8 What did you do at the weekend?

Listening comprehension

1 Mrs Bennet is talking with a friend about her recent vacation in England. Listen to their conversation and mark each statement TRUE (write T) or FALSE (write F).

 1 Mrs Bennet returned a month ago. ....
 2 She didn't visit many places in England. ....
 3 She saw some plays in London. ....
 4 She didn't have time to visit the museums. ....
 5 She often went shopping while she was there. ....
 6 She went on a bus tour in York. ....
 7 She saw many modern buildings in Oxford. ....
 8 She found there were lots of things to see in Oxford. ....
 9 The weather was cold in England. ....

2 You will hear Jim and Mary talking about what they did during the weekend. Listen to their conversation and mark in the table ☑ the things they did.

	Jim	Mary
Went to the movies		
Played tennis		
Watched TV		
Went out for dinner		

	Jim	Mary
Studied		
Went dancing		
Went swimming		

3 You will hear Kevin talking about a picnic he went on on Sunday. Listen to the conversation and write down the time at which each thing happened.

PICNIC TO GOLDEN BEACH	Time		Time
Bus departs		Explore Magic Island	
Arrive at beach		Boat returns to the beach	
Free for swimming		Free for swimming	
Boat trip to Magic Island		Bus departs	
Picnic lunch on Magic Island			

Conversation exercises

Choose the most suitable answer and write it out.

1 **A** How was your weekend?

   B ....

   | Very much.
   | Yes, it was.
   | Fine, thanks.

2 **A** Did you do anything in the weekend?

   B ....

   | Not very much.
   | Yes, very much.
   | Not at all.

3 **A** Did you have a nice holiday?

   B ....

   | Yes, a lot.
   | Yes, very pleasant.
   | Not very much.

4 **A** How was the movie?

   B ....

   | No, it wasn't.
   | Very interesting.
   | Not much.

5 **A** How was the food?

   B ....

   | No, I didn't.
   | Yes, it was.
   | It was delicious.

Grammar review

1 Answer each question with *No, there weren't very many* or *No, there wasn't very much*.

   1 Were there a lot of students at the party?

      ....

   2 Was there a lot of rain while you were on holiday?

      ....

   3 Was there plenty of food at the party?

      ....

   4 Were there a lot of cars on the road?

      ....

   5 Was there a lot of traffic on the highway?

      ....

   6 Were there a lot of tourists at the museum?

      ....

   7 Were there a lot of people at the beach?

      ....

2 Write answers to these questions using the times given.

1 What time did the concert begin? (8 o'clock)
It began at 8 o'clock.

2 When did the fire break out? (3 a.m.)
....

3 What time did the plane leave? (7 o'clock)
....

4 What time did the baby fall asleep? (6 p.m.)
....

5 What time did the baby wake up? (9 o'clock)
....

3 Write answers to these questions using the times given.

1 What time did you have lunch? (11.30)
I had lunch at half past eleven.

2 When did you feel ill? (3.30)
....

3 When did you hear the noise? (midnight)
....

4 What time did you smell smoke? (2 a.m.)
....

5 When did you buy your ticket? (4 p.m.)
....

4 Write suitable replies suggesting an alternative activity.

1 Did you go to the movies on Sunday night?
No, I didn't. I watched television instead.

2 Did you play tennis on Sunday afternoon?
....

3 Did you go out for dinner on Friday night?
....

4 Did you watch TV last night?
....

Writing

Put these sentences into the correct order and write out the composition below.

> A VISIT TO PATTAYA
> First we went to the beach and had a swim.
> We got up very early and left before the traffic became too busy.
> Last weekend I went to Pattaya with some friends.
> I bought a nice Thai painting.
> We arrived in Pattaya at about 9.30.
> The water was quite warm.
> We got back to Bangkok at about 3 o'clock.
> Pattaya is a beautiful beach about an hour and a half from Bangkok.
> We drove to Pattaya by car.
> After the boat ride we had a delicious lunch in a restaurant near the beach.
> Then it was becoming very hot so we drove back to Bangkok.
> We visited a temple and some shops.
> Then we went for a ride on a boat.
> After lunch we walked around the town for a while.

Unit 9 Have you or haven't you?

Listening comprehension

1 You will hear a tourist talking about her visit to a foreign country. Listen to the conversation and mark ☑ the places she has been to or the things she has done so far.

   Botanical Gardens ☐   Opera House ☐
   Bird Park ☐   City Hall ☐
   National Art Gallery ☐   University ☐
   Modern Art Museum ☐   Boat trip ☐

2 Eric is being interviewed about his health. Listen to the interview and mark each topic YES ☑ or NO ☒.

HEALTH QUESTIONNAIRE	Yes	No
Been hospitalized		
Had a serious illness		
Had a polio injection		
Had a TB injection		
Had any of the following diseases:		
Measles		
Tuberculosis		
Cholera		
Malaria		

3 You will hear Patricia and George talking about recent leisure activities. Mark the things they have ☑ or haven't ☒ done.

	Patricia	George
Seen a movie		
Read a novel		
Played tennis		
Eaten at a restaurant		

33

Conversation exercises

1 Choose the most suitable answer and write it out.

1 **A** When did you arrive?
  B ....
  Since Monday.
  For a week.
  On Monday.

2 **A** Have you been to the zoo yet?
  B ....
  Yes, I have.
  Yes, I did.
  No, I haven't.

3 **A** How long have you been studying English?
  B ....
  For three years.
  Since six years.
  Yes, I have.

4 **A** Have you seen the town hall yet?
  B ....
  No, I've seen it.
  Yes, I will.
  Yes, I've seen it already.

5 **A** Have you seen the museum?
  B ....
  Not yet.
  Not already.
  Not now.

6 **A** Will you be here for long?
  B ....
  Not at all.
  For a week.
  Since Monday.

2 Write answers to these questions using the information given.

1 **A** Have you been in London for long? (two weeks)
  B *I've been in London for two weeks.*

2 **A** Have you worn glasses for long? (3 years)
  B ....

3 **A** Have you been travelling for long? (a month)
  B ....

3 Now respond with *since* ... and the information given.

1 **A** How long have you been here? (Monday)
  B ....

2 **A** How long have you been studying English? (1975)
  B ....

3 **A** How long have you been feeling ill? (Monday)
  B ....

4 Write answers to these questions using a sentence in the past tense and the information given.

1 **A** Have you been to Tokyo? (1980)
  B *Yes, I went there in 1980.*

2 **A** Have you seen the movie at the Rex Cinema? (on Sunday)
  B ....

3 **A** Have you ever tried Mexican food? (in Los Angeles)
  B ....

4 **A** Have you read *War and Peace*? (at school)
  B ....

5 **A** Have you been to the gymnasium recently? (on Saturday)
  B ....

6 **A** Have you ever eaten at the Scala Restaurant? (last month)
  B ....

7 **A** Have you ever had malaria? (when I was a child)
  B ....

5 Write answers to these questions using a time phrase + *ago* (e.g. a week ago, a year ago, six months ago, etc.).

1 **A** When was the last time you went swimming?
  B ....

2 **A** When was the last time you saw a movie?
  B ....

3 **A** When was the last time you went to a restaurant?
  B ....

4 **A** When was the last time you went on vacation?
  B ....

5 **A** When was the last time you saw your grandparents?
  B ....

6 **A** When was the last time you ate seafood?
  B ....

7 **A** When was the last time you played sport?
  B ....

Writing

Read this information about a group of tourists visiting a city.

Name	Arrived	Leaving	Museum	Zoo	Golden Beach	Art Centre	Craft Centre	Mount Taba
Mr Smith	6 June	15 June		✓		✓		✓
Mrs Lee	4 June	11 June	✓		✓		✓	
Mr Fox	2 June	18 June		✓	✓			✓
Miss West	3 June	13 June	✓	✓	✓			
Mr Doe	4 June	12 June				✓	✓	✓
Mrs Kent	5 June	14 June	✓		✓		✓	

Today's date is the 10th of June. Read this paragraph about Mr Smith.

Mr Smith arrived on June 6. He has been here for four days. He is leaving on June 15. So far he has been to the Zoo, to the Art Centre, and to Mount Taba. He hasn't been to the Museum, to Golden Beach or to the Craft Centre yet.

Write paragraphs like this about the other people above.

1 ....

2 ....

3 ....

4 ....

5 ....

Unit 10   How do you do it?

Listening comprehension

1 You will hear Gillian and Anne talking about a recipe. Listen to their conversation and write down the order in which each activity takes place by writing 1, 2, 3, 4, etc., beside each phrase.

RECIPE FOR BEEF STEW

Add the red wine. ....   Fry the tomatoes and onions. ....

Take out the vegetables. ....   Add the water. ....

Cook it slowly for about two hours. ....   Put everything into a deep saucepan. ....

Fry the beef. ....   Add the spices. ....

---

2 Bill is telling Joe how to use his typewriter. Listen to his explanation and mark ☑ the correct function for each of the things he talks about.

Item   **Function**
1 The red button on the left   ☐ moves the ribbon.
                                      ☐ turns on the power.
                                      ☐ moves the paper.
2 The black button   ☐ spaces the letters.
                                      ☐ turns the paper.
                                      ☐ spaces the paper.
3 The metal rod   ☐ holds the ribbon.
                                      ☐ turns the ribbon.
                                      ☐ holds the paper.
4 The return switch   ☐ moves you on to the next line.
                                      ☐ moves the ribbon forward.
                                      ☐ types over a line.
5 The white switch   ☐ makes double spaces.
                                      ☐ erases mistakes.
                                      ☐ underlines.

3 A salesman is explaining to Mrs Johnson how to use her new washing-machine. Listen to the conversation and draw a line from the items in A to the correct items in B.

A	B
water level	round brown switch
water temperature	plastic shelf
washing timer	black switch
soap container	red switch
start button	white button
	plastic tray
	black box

37

Grammar review

1 Write these sentences out in full using this model.

1 start the engine/put the car into neutral/turn the key
   To start the engine, first put the car into neutral and then turn the key.

2 turn on the fan/put in the plug/push the blue button

3 use the cassette player/put in the batteries/put the cassette in here

4 change the film/open the back of the camera/put the new film inside

5 change the tyre/ remove the hubcap/take off the wheel nuts

6 cook rice/ wash the rice/ cook it slowly for 20 minutes

2 Now use this model.

1 What do I do after I cut up the vegetables? (fry them)
   After you cut up the vegetables you fry them.

2 What do I do after I wash the rice? (cover it with water)

3 What do I do after I cut up the meat? (fry it)

4 What do I do after I prepare the chicken? (put it in the oven)

5 What do I do after I prepare the meat? (prepare the salad)

3 Write answers to these questions using this model.

1 What's the red button for? (wind on the film)
The red button is for winding on the film.

2 What's this metal part for? (attach the flash)
....

3 What's this metal switch for? (lock the camera)
....

4 What's this round part for? (focus the picture)
....

5 What's this lever for? (rewind the film)
....

6 What's this numbered part for? (adjust the lens)
....

7 What's this plastic cover for? (cover the lens)
....

4 Now use this model.

1 What's this switch for? (open the back of the cassette player)
It's to open the back of the cassette player.

2 What's this button for? (rewind the cassette)
....

3 What's this red switch for? (make a recording)
....

4 What's this button for? (adjust the tone)
....

5 What's the grey switch for? (adjust the volume)
....

6 What's this part here for? (plug in the microphone)
....

7 What's this button for? (fast forward the tape)
....

Writing

Read this recipe for tomato soup.

Tomato Soup

Ingredients	Method
4 large tomatoes	1 Cut the tomatoes, onions and garlic into small pieces.
1 small onion	
8 cups water	2 Fry together in a saucepan with butter for 5 minutes.
small piece garlic	
½ teaspoon salt	3 Add water, spices, salt and pepper.
¼ teaspoon pepper	4 Heat until the water boils.
saucepan with lid	5 Turn down the heat and cook gently for one hour.
½ teaspoon butter	

Read this description based on the information above. (Notice the differences between the written description below and the recipe notes above.)

To cook tomato soup you will need four large tomatoes, one small onion, eight cups of water, a small piece of garlic, half a teaspoon of salt, a quarter of a teaspoon of pepper, a saucepan with a lid and half a teaspoon of butter. First, cut up the tomatoes, the onions and the garlic into small pieces. Then fry these in a saucepan with a little butter for about five minutes. After that, add the water, the spices, the salt and the pepper. Then heat it until the water boils. Now turn down the heat and cook it gently for one hour.

Now read these recipe notes and write a description based on them like the one above.

Egg and Lemon Soup

Ingredients	Method
3 pints chicken stock	1 Put stock into saucepan and heat until boiling.
3 ounces rice	
4 eggs, well beaten	2 Add rice and cook on low heat for 15 minutes.
juice of 2 lemons	
salt and pepper	3 Mix together egg and lemon juice.
saucepan	4 Add 3 tablespoons of stock to the mixture and stir.
	5 Stir this mixture into the remaining stock in the saucepan.
	6 Add a little salt and pepper.
	7 Cook gently for 3 minutes.

Unit 11 What do I need to do?

Listening comprehension

1 Richard is planning to study in Australia. He is talking to a counsellor at the Embassy about what he must do. Listen to their conversation and mark whether the statements below are TRUE (write T) or FALSE (write F).

1 He has to return to the Embassy in a week. ....

2 He should come with his parents. ....

3 His parents must sign a paper. ....

4 He has to bring a bank statement. ....

5 He will have to bring several medical documents. ....

6 He must bring his school transcripts. ....

7 He needs to get a letter of recommendation. ....

8 He should buy some warm clothes before he leaves. ....

2 Gillian is telling Leslie how to prepare a fish dish. Listen to their conversation and mark ☑ on the lists below the things that Leslie needs to remember to do.

Things to buy

☐ prawns
☐ fish
☐ pork
☐ vegetables

Instructions

☐ Fry the fish.
☐ Fry the vegetables.
☐ Add some saffron spice.
☐ Add salt.
☐ Clean the prawns.

☐ Take off the prawn tails.
☐ Buy a sweet red wine.
☐ Buy a dry white wine.
☐ Don't add any water.
☐ Cook it for at least an hour.

3 You will hear Karen talking to a customs officer about what she is allowed to take into the country without paying a tax on it. Listen to their conversation and mark ☑ the correct information in the table.

Item	Quantity			
Liquor	1 ☐	2 ☐	3 ☐ BOTTLES	
Cigarettes	200 ☐	300 ☐	400 ☐	
US Dollars	$500 ☐	$1,500 ☐	$2,500 ☐	$5,000 ☐
Watches	0 ☐	1 ☐	2 ☐ 3 ☐ 4 ☐	
Radios	0 ☐	1 ☐	2 ☐ 3 ☐ 4 ☐	
Cameras	0 ☐	1 ☐	2 ☐ 3 ☐ 4 ☐	

Grammar review

1 Write answers to these questions using the information given and this model.

1 What do I need to do? (fill out this form)
You will have to fill out this form.

2 How long will I have to wait? (about two weeks)
....

3 What do I need to bring? (two passport photographs)
....

4 How much will I need to pay? (twenty-five dollars)
....

5 What clothing will I need to take? (warm clothing)
....

6 When will I need to report at the airport? (8 o'clock)
....

7 Where will I have to wait? (in the waiting lounge)
....

2 Now reply using *not allowed to...* and this model.

1 Can I take food into the library?
No, you're not allowed to take food into the library.

2 Is it all right to take my bag into the library?
....

3 Can I borrow more than five books at once?
....

4 Is it all right to keep books for more than two weeks?
....

5 Can I borrow books for other people?
....

6 Is it all right to lend my card to someone else?
....

7 Can I borrow magazines?
....

3 Look at this sign.
This means:
You must not park here between 9 a.m. and 12 a.m.
OR
You cannot park here between 9 a.m. and 12 a.m.
OR
You are not allowed to park here between 9 a.m. and 12 a.m.

Write a sentence explaining what these signs mean.

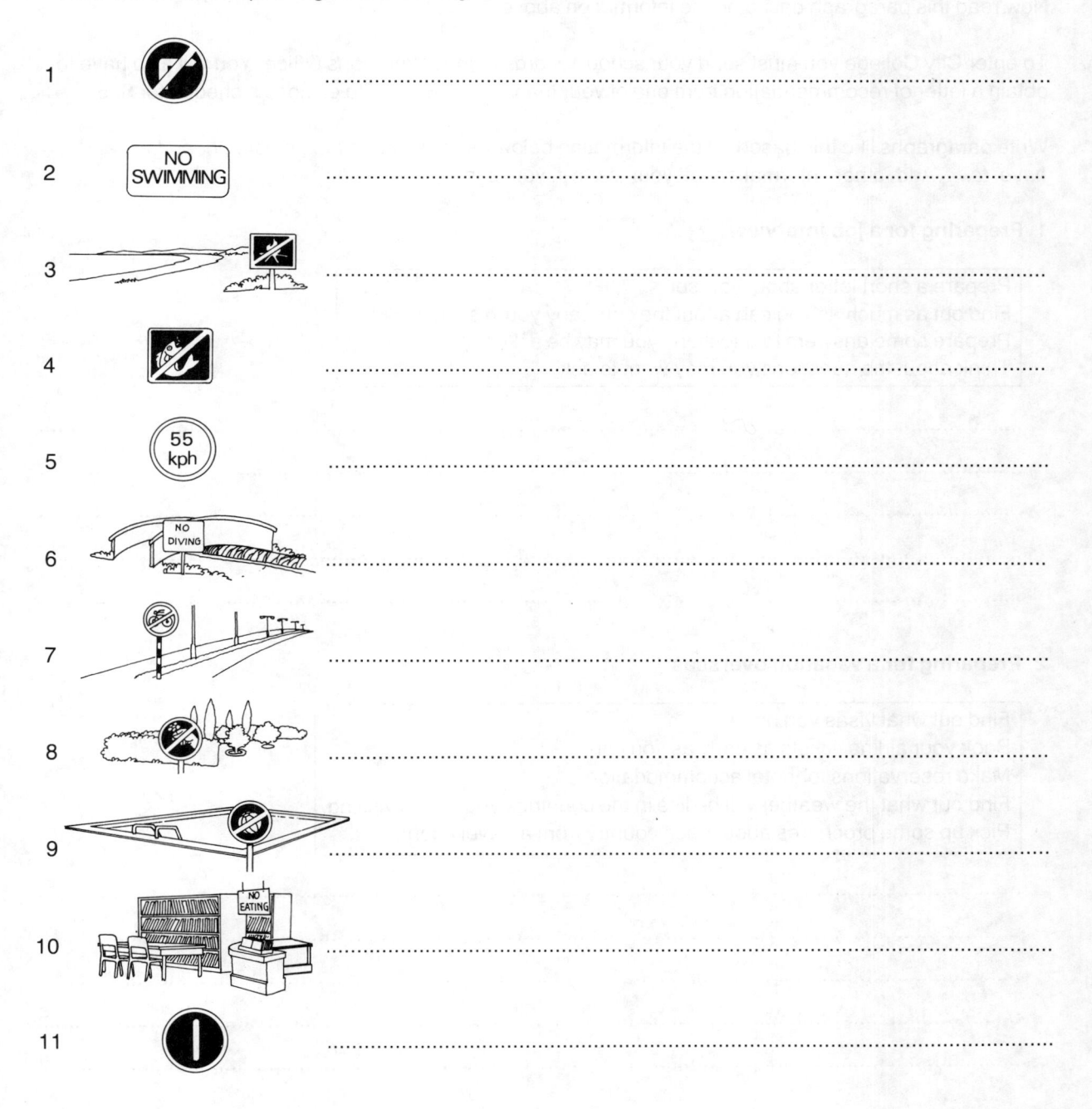

1 ....

2 ....

3 ....

4 ....

5 ....

6 ....

7 ....

8 ....

9 ....

10 ....

11 ....

Writing

Read the list of things that you need to do when applying for admission to City College.

- send your school records to the Admissions Office
- obtain a letter of recommendation from one of your teachers
- enclose a cheque for $25

Now read this paragraph based on the information above.

To enter City College you must send your school records to the Admissions Office. You will also have to obtain a letter of recommendation from one of your teachers. You need to enclose a cheque for $25.

Write paragraphs like this based on the information below using *will have to...*; *must...*; *need to...*; and *have to....* Add other information of your own if you can.

1 Preparing for a job interview

Prepare a short letter about yourself.
Find out as much as you can about the company you wish to work for.
Prepare some answers to questions you may be asked.
Think about the questions you may want to ask.

....
....
....
....
....

2 Preparing for a vacation overseas

Find out what visas you need.
Book your airline tickets as early as you can.
Make reservations for hotel accommodation.
Find out what the weather will be like in the countries you will be visiting.
Pick up some brochures about each country from a travel agent.

....
....
....
....
....

Unit 12 What could it be?

Listening comprehension

1 You will hear people discussing different situations. Listen to each possibility and then mark ☑ the one they agree on.

1 a Dad is working late at the office. ☐
   b He stopped off at the gymnasium to play squash. ☐
   c He must have had an accident. ☐
   d He must have got delayed in the traffic. ☐

2 a She left her dictionary in the cafeteria. ☐
   b She must have left it at home. ☐
   c She left it in the English class. ☐
   d She left it in the library. ☐

3 a She didn't follow the recipe. ☐
   b She didn't use the right spices. ☐
   c She forgot to add salt. ☐
   d She cooked it for too long. ☐

4 a The cassette player hasn't got any batteries in it. ☐
   b It needs new batteries. ☐
   c The cassette hasn't been put in properly. ☐
   d The starter button is damaged. ☐

2 You will hear people talking about different items in a department store. Listen to each conversation and mark ☑ the things they are talking about.

1 a vegetable slicer   ☐
   a meat slicer   ☐
   an egg slicer   ☐
   a bread slicer   ☐

2 a medical instrument ☐
   a plant feeder   ☐
   a garden tool   ☐
   a meat thermometer   ☐

3 a coat hanger   ☐
   a book holder   ☐
   a kitchen tool   ☐
   a garden tool   ☐

Conversation exercises

1 Write answers to these statements using the information given and this model.

1. **A** I can't find my car keys. (in the car)
   B *You must have left them in the car.*

2. **A** I can't find my dictionary. (in the library)
   B ....

3. **A** I can't find my glasses. (at the swimming-pool)
   B ....

4. **A** I can't find my bag. (in the taxi)
   B ....

5. **A** I can't find my wallet. (at home)
   B ....

6. **A** I can't find my address book. (at the office)
   B ....

7. **A** I can't find my driving-licence. (in the car)
   B ....

2 Write answers to these statements suggesting where each item could be. The first one is done for you.

1. **A** I wonder where my keys are. (in the car)
   B *Do you think they could be in the car?*

2. **A** I wonder where my dictionary is.
   B ....

3. **A** I wonder where my sunglasses are.
   B ....

4. **A** I wonder where my fountain pen is.
   B ....

5. **A** I wonder where the telephone directory is.
   B ....

6. **A** I wonder where my shoes are.
   B ....

7. **A** I wonder where my briefcase is.
   B ....

3 Suggest what went wrong with the following dishes. Use the model below. Use some of the phrases in the box or add other suggestions of your own.

> cooked it too long; used the wrong recipe; used too much salt; not used enough water; not used enough spices; forgotten to add salt; forgotten to add any spices

1 **A** I wonder what's wrong with this cake. It's not very soft.
  B *Perhaps you may have used too much flour.*

2 **A** I wonder why this fish doesn't taste very nice.
  B ....

3 **A** I wonder why this beef is so tough.
  B ....

4 **A** I wonder why this soup tastes so watery.
  B ....

5 **A** I wonder why this chicken is so dry.
  B ....

6 **A** I wonder why this coffee tastes so bitter.
  B ....

7 **A** I wonder why these vegetables are so tasteless.
  B ....

8 **A** I wonder why this rice is so dry.
  B ....

9 **A** I wonder why this soup doesn't taste very nice.
  B ....

10 **A** I wonder why this curry tastes so hot.
   B ....

11 **A** I wonder why this soup tastes so sweet.
   B ....

12 **A** I wonder why this cake tastes so strange.
   B ....

13 **A** I wonder why this egg is so tough.
   B ....

14 **A** I wonder why this dish tastes so oily.
   B ....

Writing

Read these notes about the defective record-player.

worn out motor?
faulty connection?
broken turntable belt?

Now read this note.

> Several things may be wrong with the record-player.
> First, the motor could be worn out. There could be a faulty connection as well. In addition, the turntable belt could be broken.

Write notes like this about these items based on the information given.

1.
tube—worn out?
TV aerial—damaged?
faulty electric cable?

....

....

....

....

2.
petrol supply—blocked?
dirty spark-plugs?
battery—dead?
broken starter?

....

....

....

....

3.
burned out motor?
electric cable—damaged?
keys—jammed?

....

....

....

....

Unit 13 What's it like there?

Listening comprehension

1 You will hear Rudolph talking to Vernon about his home town. Listen to their conversation and mark TRUE ☑ or FALSE ☒ beside each statement.

1 His town is near the sea. TRUE ☐ FALSE ☐
2 He comes from quite a small town. TRUE ☐ FALSE ☐
3 It is a modern city. TRUE ☐ FALSE ☐
4 There is a lot of tourism. TRUE ☐ FALSE ☐
5 There is a lot of industry. TRUE ☐ FALSE ☐
6 There is a small museum. TRUE ☐ FALSE ☐
7 The mountains are covered with snow in winter. TRUE ☐ FALSE ☐
8 It has a cold winter. TRUE ☐ FALSE ☐
9 It is a good place for shopping. TRUE ☐ FALSE ☐

2 You will hear a tourist at the airport talking to someone at the information counter. Listen to their conversation and complete the information in the table below.

Distance to the city:	.... kilometres	**Things to see:** (Mark ☑ the things mentioned)	
Time taken:	.... minutes		
Transport: (Mark ☑ what is available)		shopping	
	bus	art gallery	
	train	old buildings	
	subway	museum	
	taxi	castle	
Hotels:		craft centre	
Expensive hotel	.... dollars		
Medium hotel	.... dollars		
Inexpensive hotel	.... dollars		

3 You will hear Jane and Susan talking about the weather in Susan's home town. Listen to their conversation and complete the information in the table below.

Summer months: ☐ November ☐ December ☐ January ☐ February ☐ March ☐ April
Winter months: ☐ May ☐ June ☐ July ☐ August ☐ September ☐ October
Summer weather: ☐ hot and dry ☐ hot and wet ☐ warm and humid ☐ warm and wet
Winter weather: ☐ cool and wet ☐ cold and windy ☐ dry and cold ☐ cold with snow
Warmest temperature in summer: ....
Coldest temperature in winter: ....

Conversation exercises

1 Write answers to these questions using the information given and this model.

1. **A** What's Tokyo like? (large city/excellent subway/good restaurants)
   B *Tokyo's a large city with an excellent subway and with good restaurants.*

2. **A** What's Chicago like? (interesting/lots of skyscrapers/beautiful lakeside apartments)
   B ....

3. **A** Tell me about San Fransisco. (beautiful/large old Victorian houses/very good restaurants)
   B ....

4. **A** What's Hawaii like? (small place/beautiful scenery/good beaches)
   B ....

5. **A** Tell me about Hong Kong. (fascinating/wonderful harbour/great shops and restaurants)
   B ....

6. **A** What's London like? (charming/good shops/interesting buildings/lovely parks)
   B ....

7. **A** Tell me about Singapore. (very clean/lots of shopping centres/good restaurants)
   B ....

8. **A** What's Paris like? (beautiful/charming buildings/excellent restaurants)
   B ....

9. **A** Tell me about Bangkok. (rather hot and crowded/interesting temples/good shopping)
   B ....

10. **A** And what's Los Angeles like? (huge/lots of museums/great night-clubs)
    B ....

2 Reply to these questions using this model.

1 **A** What's Bangkok best known for? (food/friendly people)
   B *It's best known for its food and its friendly people.*

2 **A** What's New York best known for? (theatres/shops)
   B ....

3 **A** What's Hawaii best known for? (climate/great beaches)
   B ....

4 **A** What's Tokyo best known for? (night-clubs/shopping)
   B ....

5 **A** What's London best known for? (historical buildings/shops)
   B ....

6 **A** What's Hong Kong best known for? (harbour/restaurants)
   B ....

7 **A** What's Sydney best known for? (Opera House/beaches)
   B ....

3 Write sentences like the above about four cities or towns that you know saying what they are best known for.

1 ....
2 ....
3 ....
4 ....

4 Look at this sentence.

One of the best things to do in Hong Kong is to take a harbour cruise.

Write sentences like this about other cities or towns you know.

1 ....
....
2 ....
....
3 ....
....

Writing

Read this paragraph about Singapore.

The airport in Singapore is called Changi International Airport. It is about 16 kilometres from the city. You can take a taxi from the airport to the city. It costs about $10. Hotels in Singapore cost from about $50 a day upwards. Singapore has many tourist attractions. There are good shops, restaurants, and night-clubs. One of the best things to do is to take a bus tour around the island. The best time to visit Singapore is from September to December when the weather is not quite so hot.

Write a paragraph like this about Honolulu based on this information.

- airport—Honolulu International Airport
- 5 miles from city
- taxis/buses available
- taxi – $10; bus $2
- hotels from $15 – $200
- attractions: beaches, tours, restaurants, Hawaiian music and dancing
- evening sunset dinner cruise on the ocean is very good
- weather good all year; wetter from November to end January

Now write a paragraph like this about your capital city or any city you know.

Unit 14 What should I do?

Listening comprehension

1 James is visiting the doctor. Listen to the doctor's advice and mark the things that James should ☑ or shouldn't ☒ do.

   1 He should take the red pills with water. ☐

   2 He should drink strong coffee. ☐

   3 The yellow tablets should be taken in the morning. ☐

   4 The yellow tablets are very strong. ☐

   5 He shouldn't eat oily food while taking the medicine. ☐

   6 He may drink alcohol if he wishes. ☐

2 Jean and Paul are getting ready to go away for a short vacation at the seaside. Listen to their conversation and mark ☑ on the list the things they decide to take with them.

   ☐ bathroom towels   ☐ raincoats

   ☐ beach towels   ☐ umbrellas

   ☐ shampoo   ☐ food to eat on the way

   ☐ soap   ☐ cheque-books

   ☐ warm sweaters   ☐ lots of cash

3 Gary has just bought a new car. The salesperson is giving him advice about how to look after it. Listen to their conversation and complete the information in the table below.

   1 Check the batteries every .... months.

   2 Change the oil every .... months.

   3 Check the water in the radiator every .... months.

   4 Check the tyres every .... months.

   5 Tyre pressure should be .... pounds.

   6 Bring the car in for first servicing after .... thousand miles.

   7 Bring the car in for second servicing after .... thousand miles.

Conversation exercises

1 Choose the best response and write it out.

1 **A** Why don't you get something from the doctor?

   B ....

   I guess so.
   I guess I should.
   I guess not.

2 **A** You had better not go to work today.

   B ....

   Yes, I will.
   I suppose so.
   I guess not.

3 **A** You ought to go on a diet.

   B ....

   I don't think it's necessary.
   I suppose not.
   No, I will.

4 **A** Have you thought about taking English lessons?

   B ....

   Why not?
   Yes, I guess I should.
   It's OK.

5 **A** You shouldn't put your bike there.

   B ....

   Yes, I will.
   Yes, maybe.
   No, I won't.

2 Make alternative suggestions as responses using this model.

1 **A** Can I park my car in front of your house?

   B *No, you had better park it at the back of the house.*

2 **A** Can I wash this shirt in hot water?

   B ....

3 **A** Can I clean this record with alcohol?

   B ....

4 **A** Can I wear this shirt with a green tie?

   B ....

5 **A** Can I eat my lunch in the library?

   B ....

6 **A** Can I wear short pants to the party?

   B ....

7 **A** Can I give in my homework on Friday?

   B ....

8 **A** Can I take this medicine with coffee?

   B ....

54

3 Make suggestions using the information given and this model.

1 **A** I've got an awful headache. (take something for it)
  B *Perhaps you ought to take something for it.*

2 **A** I feel quite exhausted. (take a few days rest)
  B ....

3 **A** I wish I could make more friends. (join a club)
  B ....

4 **A** I wish I could type. (take a course)
  B ....

5 **A** I really need to lose some weight. (go on a diet)
  B ....

6 **A** I've got a very sore throat. (take some Vitamin C)
  B ....

7 **A** I need to get more exercise. (take up a sport)
  B ....

8 **A** I wish I knew something about photography. (join a camera club)
  B ....

4 Make suggestions of your own using *Well, why don't you ...?*

1 **A** I wish I knew how to drive.
  B ....

2 **A** I wish I could improve my English.
  B ....

3 **A** I need to put on weight. I'm too thin.
  B ....

4 **A** I've got a very painful tooth.
  B ....

5 **A** I think the engine of my car needs checking.
  B ....

6 **A** My hair is really far too long.
  B ....

7 **A** I wish I could get more exercise.
  B ....

Writing

Read these instructions for looking after a record-player.

> - clean your records before using them
> - don't use a damaged needle
> - change the needle regularly
> - don't keep the record-player in a hot place

Read this paragraph based on the notes above.

> Remember that you need to clean your records before using them. Don't forget that you mustn't use a damaged needle. Remember that you ought to change the needle regularly. Finally, don't forget that you shouldn't keep the record-player in a hot place.

Write paragraphs like this based on the notes below.

1 **Looking after your motorcycle**
   - keep it clean at all times
   - park it carefully
   - don't leave it unlocked
   - clean the spark-plugs regularly
   - don't use poor grade petrol

   ....
   ....
   ....

2 **Looking after your new electric typewriter**
   - clean the keys regularly
   - keep the cover on it when you are not using it
   - don't let it get damp or wet
   - make sure the plug is always properly connected
   - don't drop it or put it down heavily

   ....
   ....
   ....

3 **Looking after your new camera**
   - don't clean the lens with alcohol; use a dry cloth
   - put the lens cover on when you are not using it
   - don't get sand or dirt on it
   - keep it in a cool place when there is a film in it
   - take the film out in a dark place

   ....
   ....
   ....